Date _____

MEALS:
BREAKFAST

LUNCH

DINNER

PRIORITIES

APPOINTMENTS

WATER

○ ○ ○
○ ○ ○
○ ○

CLEAN
THE
HOUSE

WORDS TO
LIVE BY

TO DO

THINGS
TO BUY

NOTES

Date: _ _ _ _ _ / _ _

MEALS:
BREAKFAST

LUNCH

DINNER

PRIORITIES

WATER
○ ○ ○
○ ○ ○
○ ○

APPOINTMENTS

CLEAN THE HOUSE

WORDS TO LIVE BY

TO DO

THINGS TO BUY

NOTES

Date: _ _ _ _ _ / _ _

MEALS:
BREAKFAST

LUNCH

DINNER

PRIORITIES

APPOINTMENTS

WORDS TO LIVE BY

TO DO

NOTES

WATER

○ ○ ○
○ ○ ○
○ ○

CLEAN THE HOUSE

THINGS TO BUY

Date: _ _ _ _ _ / _ _

MEALS:
BREAKFAST

LUNCH

DINNER

PRIORITIES
_____
_____
_____
_____

APPOINTMENTS
_____
_____
_____

WATER
○ ○ ○
○ ○ ○
○ ○

CLEAN THE HOUSE

WORDS TO LIVE BY

TO DO
_____
_____
_____
_____
_____
_____
_____

THINGS TO BUY

NOTES
_____
_____
_____
_____
_____
_____

Date: _ _ _ _ _ / _ _

PRIORITIES

MEALS:

BREAKFAST

LUNCH

DINNER

WATER

○ ○ ○
○ ○ ○
○ ○

APPOINTMENTS

CLEAN THE HOUSE

WORDS TO LIVE BY

TO DO

THINGS TO BUY

NOTES

Date: _ _ _ _ _ / _ _

PRIORITIES

MEALS:

BREAKFAST

LUNCH

DINNER

WATER

○ ○ ○
○ ○ ○
○ ○

APPOINTMENTS

CLEAN THE HOUSE

WORDS TO LIVE BY

TO DO

THINGS TO BUY

NOTES

Date: _ _ _ _ _ / _ _

MEALS:

BREAKFAST

LUNCH

DINNER

PRIORITIES

APPOINTMENTS

WORDS TO LIVE BY

TO DO

NOTES

WATER

○ ○ ○
○ ○ ○
○ ○

CLEAN THE HOUSE

THINGS TO BUY

Date: _ _ _ _ _ / _ _

MEALS:
BREAKFAST

LUNCH

DINNER

PRIORITIES

APPOINTMENTS

WORDS TO LIVE BY

TO DO

NOTES

WATER

○ ○ ○
○ ○ ○
○ ○

CLEAN THE HOUSE

THINGS TO BUY

Date: _ _ _ _ _ / _ _

MEALS:
BREAKFAST

LUNCH

DINNER

PRIORITIES

APPOINTMENTS

WATER
○ ○ ○
○ ○ ○
○ ○

CLEAN THE HOUSE

WORDS TO LIVE BY

TO DO

THINGS TO BUY

NOTES

Date: _ _ _ _ _ / _ _

MEALS:
BREAKFAST

LUNCH

DINNER

PRIORITIES

APPOINTMENTS

WATER

○ ○ ○
○ ○ ○
○ ○

CLEAN THE HOUSE

WORDS TO LIVE BY

TO DO

THINGS TO BUY

NOTES

Date: _ _ _ _ _ / _ _

MEALS:
BREAKFAST

LUNCH

DINNER

PRIORITIES
_____
_____
_____
_____
_____

APPOINTMENTS
_____
_____
_____
_____
_____

WATER
○ ○ ○
○ ○ ○
○ ○

CLEAN THE HOUSE

WORDS TO LIVE BY

TO DO
_____
_____
_____
_____
_____
_____
_____
_____

THINGS TO BUY

NOTES
_____
_____
_____
_____
_____
_____
_____
_____

Date: _____ / __

MEALS:
BREAKFAST

LUNCH

DINNER

PRIORITIES
_____
_____
_____
_____

WATER
◯ ◯ ◯
◯ ◯ ◯
◯ ◯

APPOINTMENTS
_____
_____
_____

CLEAN THE HOUSE

WORDS TO LIVE BY

TO DO
_____
_____
_____
_____
_____
_____
_____
_____
_____
_____
_____
_____
_____
_____
_____
_____

THINGS TO BUY

NOTES

Date: _ _ _ _ _ / _ _

MEALS:

BREAKFAST

LUNCH

DINNER

PRIORITIES

APPOINTMENTS

WORDS TO LIVE BY

TO DO

NOTES

WATER

○ ○ ○
○ ○ ○
○ ○

CLEAN THE HOUSE

THINGS TO BUY

Date: _ _ _ _ _ / _ _

MEALS:

BREAKFAST

LUNCH

DINNER

PRIORITIES

APPOINTMENTS

WORDS TO LIVE BY

TO DO

NOTES

WATER

◯ ◯ ◯
◯ ◯ ◯
◯ ◯

CLEAN THE HOUSE

THINGS TO BUY

Date: _ _ _ _ _ / _ _

MEALS:

BREAKFAST

LUNCH

DINNER

PRIORITIES

WATER

○ ○ ○
○ ○ ○
○ ○

APPOINTMENTS

CLEAN THE HOUSE

WORDS TO LIVE BY

TO DO

THINGS TO BUY

NOTES

Date: _ _ _ _ _ / _ _

MEALS:

BREAKFAST

LUNCH

DINNER

PRIORITIES

APPOINTMENTS

WATER

○ ○ ○
○ ○ ○
○ ○

CLEAN THE HOUSE

WORDS TO LIVE BY

TO DO

THINGS TO BUY

NOTES

Date: _ _ _ _ _ / _ _

MEALS:
BREAKFAST

LUNCH

DINNER

PRIORITIES
_____
_____
_____
_____
_____

WATER
○ ○ ○
○ ○ ○
○ ○

APPOINTMENTS
_____
_____
_____
_____

CLEAN THE HOUSE

WORDS TO LIVE BY

TO DO
_____
_____
_____
_____
_____
_____
_____
_____

THINGS TO BUY

NOTES
_____
_____
_____
_____
_____
_____
_____

Date: _ _ _ _ _ / _ _

MEALS:
BREAKFAST

LUNCH

DINNER

PRIORITIES

APPOINTMENTS

WATER

○ ○ ○
○ ○ ○
○ ○

CLEAN THE HOUSE

WORDS TO LIVE BY

TO DO

THINGS TO BUY

NOTES

Date: _ _ _ _ _ / _ _

MEALS:

BREAKFAST

LUNCH

DINNER

PRIORITIES

APPOINTMENTS

WATER

○ ○ ○
○ ○ ○
○ ○

CLEAN THE HOUSE

WORDS TO LIVE BY

TO DO

THINGS TO BUY

NOTES

Date: _ _ _ _ _ / _ _

MEALS:
BREAKFAST

LUNCH

DINNER

PRIORITIES

APPOINTMENTS

WATER

○ ○ ○
○ ○ ○
○ ○

CLEAN THE HOUSE

WORDS TO LIVE BY

TO DO

THINGS TO BUY

NOTES

Date: _ _ _ _ _ / _ _

MEALS:
BREAKFAST

LUNCH

DINNER

PRIORITIES

APPOINTMENTS

WATER

○ ○ ○
○ ○ ○
○ ○

CLEAN THE HOUSE

WORDS TO LIVE BY

TO DO

THINGS TO BUY

NOTES

Date: _____ / __

MEALS:
BREAKFAST

LUNCH

DINNER

PRIORITIES
_____
_____
_____

WATER
○ ○ ○
○ ○ ○
○ ○

APPOINTMENTS
_____
_____
_____
_____

CLEAN THE HOUSE

WORDS TO LIVE BY

TO DO
_____
_____
_____
_____
_____
_____
_____

THINGS TO BUY

NOTES
_____
_____
_____
_____
_____
_____

Date: _ _ _ _ _ / _ _

MEALS:
BREAKFAST

LUNCH

DINNER

PRIORITIES

APPOINTMENTS

WORDS TO LIVE BY

TO DO

NOTES

WATER

○ ○ ○
○ ○ ○
○ ○

CLEAN THE HOUSE

THINGS TO BUY

Date: _ _ _ _ _ / _ _

MEALS:

BREAKFAST

LUNCH

DINNER

PRIORITIES

_____
_____
_____
_____

APPOINTMENTS

_____
_____
_____
_____

WATER

○ ○ ○
○ ○ ○
○ ○

CLEAN THE HOUSE

WORDS TO LIVE BY

TO DO

_____
_____
_____
_____
_____
_____
_____
_____
_____
_____
_____
_____
_____
_____
_____

THINGS TO BUY

NOTES

Date: _ _ _ _ _ / _ _

MEALS:
BREAKFAST

LUNCH

DINNER

PRIORITIES

APPOINTMENTS

WORDS TO LIVE BY

TO DO

NOTES

WATER

○ ○ ○
○ ○ ○
○ ○

CLEAN THE HOUSE

THINGS TO BUY

Date: _ _ _ _ _ / _ _

MEALS:
BREAKFAST

LUNCH

DINNER

PRIORITIES

APPOINTMENTS

WATER

○ ○ ○
○ ○ ○
○ ○

CLEAN THE HOUSE

WORDS TO LIVE BY

TO DO

THINGS TO BUY

NOTES

Date: _ _ _ _ _ / _ _

MEALS:

BREAKFAST

LUNCH

DINNER

PRIORITIES

APPOINTMENTS

WATER

○ ○ ○
○ ○ ○
○ ○

**CLEAN
THE
HOUSE**

**WORDS TO
LIVE BY**

TO DO

**THINGS
TO BUY**

NOTES

Date: _____ / __

MEALS:
BREAKFAST

LUNCH

DINNER

PRIORITIES

APPOINTMENTS

WATER
○ ○ ○
○ ○ ○
○ ○

CLEAN THE HOUSE

WORDS TO LIVE BY

TO DO

THINGS TO BUY

NOTES

Date: _ _ _ _ _ / _ _

PRIORITIES

MEALS:

BREAKFAST

LUNCH

DINNER

WATER

○ ○ ○
○ ○ ○
○ ○

APPOINTMENTS

CLEAN THE HOUSE

WORDS TO LIVE BY

TO DO

THINGS TO BUY

NOTES

Date: _ _ _ _ _ / _ _

MEALS:

BREAKFAST

LUNCH

DINNER

PRIORITIES

_____
_____
_____
_____
_____

APPOINTMENTS

_____
_____
_____
_____
_____

WORDS TO LIVE BY

TO DO

_____
_____
_____
_____
_____
_____
_____
_____

NOTES

_____
_____
_____
_____
_____
_____
_____

WATER

◯ ◯ ◯
◯ ◯ ◯
◯ ◯

CLEAN THE HOUSE

THINGS TO BUY

Date: _ _ _ _ _ / _ _

MEALS:
BREAKFAST

LUNCH

DINNER

PRIORITIES

APPOINTMENTS

WATER

○ ○ ○
○ ○ ○
○ ○

CLEAN THE HOUSE

WORDS TO LIVE BY

TO DO

THINGS TO BUY

NOTES

Date: _____ / __

MEALS:
BREAKFAST

LUNCH

DINNER

PRIORITIES

APPOINTMENTS

WATER
○ ○ ○
○ ○ ○
○ ○

CLEAN THE HOUSE

WORDS TO LIVE BY

TO DO

THINGS TO BUY

NOTES

Date: _ _ _ _ _ / _ _

MEALS:
BREAKFAST

LUNCH

DINNER

PRIORITIES

APPOINTMENTS

WORDS TO LIVE BY

TO DO

NOTES

WATER

○ ○ ○
○ ○ ○
○ ○

CLEAN THE HOUSE

THINGS TO BUY

Date: _ _ _ _ _ / _ _

MEALS:
BREAKFAST

LUNCH

DINNER

PRIORITIES

APPOINTMENTS

WATER

○ ○ ○
○ ○ ○
○ ○

CLEAN THE HOUSE

WORDS TO LIVE BY

TO DO

THINGS TO BUY

NOTES

Date: _____ / __

MEALS:
BREAKFAST

LUNCH

DINNER

PRIORITIES

APPOINTMENTS

WATER

○ ○ ○
○ ○ ○
○ ○

CLEAN THE HOUSE

WORDS TO LIVE BY

TO DO

THINGS TO BUY

NOTES

Date: _ _ _ _ _ / _ _

MEALS:
BREAKFAST

LUNCH

DINNER

PRIORITIES

_____
_____
_____
_____

APPOINTMENTS

_____
_____
_____
_____

WORDS TO LIVE BY

TO DO

_____
_____
_____
_____
_____
_____
_____

NOTES

_____
_____
_____
_____
_____

WATER

◯ ◯ ◯
◯ ◯ ◯
◯ ◯

CLEAN THE HOUSE

THINGS TO BUY

Date: _ _ _ _ _ / _ _

MEALS:
BREAKFAST

LUNCH

DINNER

PRIORITIES

WATER

◯ ◯ ◯
◯ ◯ ◯
◯ ◯

APPOINTMENTS

CLEAN THE HOUSE

WORDS TO LIVE BY

TO DO

THINGS TO BUY

NOTES

Date: _ _ _ _ _ / _ _

MEALS:
BREAKFAST

LUNCH

DINNER

PRIORITIES

WATER

○ ○ ○
○ ○ ○
○ ○

APPOINTMENTS

CLEAN THE HOUSE

WORDS TO LIVE BY

TO DO

THINGS TO BUY

NOTES

Date: _ _ _ _ _ / _ _

MEALS:

BREAKFAST

LUNCH

DINNER

PRIORITIES

APPOINTMENTS

WATER

○ ○ ○
○ ○ ○
○ ○

CLEAN THE HOUSE

WORDS TO LIVE BY

TO DO

THINGS TO BUY

NOTES

Date: _____ / __

MEALS:
BREAKFAST

LUNCH

DINNER

PRIORITIES
_____
_____
_____
_____

APPOINTMENTS
_____
_____
_____
_____

WATER
◯ ◯ ◯
◯ ◯ ◯
◯ ◯

CLEAN THE HOUSE

WORDS TO LIVE BY

TO DO
_____
_____
_____
_____
_____
_____
_____
_____
_____
_____
_____
_____
_____
_____
_____

THINGS TO BUY

NOTES

Date: _ _ _ _ _ / _ _

MEALS:

BREAKFAST

LUNCH

DINNER

PRIORITIES

APPOINTMENTS

WATER

○ ○ ○
○ ○ ○
○ ○

CLEAN THE HOUSE

WORDS TO LIVE BY

TO DO

THINGS TO BUY

NOTES

Date: _ _ _ _ _ / _ _

PRIORITIES

WATER

○ ○ ○
○ ○ ○
○ ○

MEALS:

BREAKFAST

LUNCH

DINNER

APPOINTMENTS

CLEAN THE HOUSE

WORDS TO LIVE BY

TO DO

THINGS TO BUY

NOTES

Date: _ _ _ _ _ / _ _

MEALS:

BREAKFAST

LUNCH

DINNER

PRIORITIES

_____
_____
_____
_____

APPOINTMENTS

_____
_____
_____
_____

WORDS TO LIVE BY

TO DO

_____
_____
_____
_____
_____
_____
_____
_____
_____

NOTES

_____
_____
_____
_____
_____

WATER

○ ○ ○
○ ○ ○
○ ○

CLEAN THE HOUSE

THINGS TO BUY

Date: _ _ _ _ _ / _ _

MEALS:
BREAKFAST

LUNCH

DINNER

PRIORITIES

APPOINTMENTS

WORDS TO LIVE BY

TO DO

NOTES

WATER

○ ○ ○
○ ○ ○
○ ○

CLEAN THE HOUSE

THINGS TO BUY

Date: _ _ _ _ _ / _ _

MEALS:
BREAKFAST

LUNCH

DINNER

PRIORITIES

APPOINTMENTS

WATER

○ ○ ○
○ ○ ○
○ ○

CLEAN THE HOUSE

WORDS TO LIVE BY

TO DO

THINGS TO BUY

NOTES

Date: _ _ _ _ _ / _ _

MEALS:
BREAKFAST

LUNCH

DINNER

PRIORITIES

APPOINTMENTS

WATER

◯ ◯ ◯
◯ ◯ ◯
◯ ◯

CLEAN THE HOUSE

WORDS TO LIVE BY

TO DO

THINGS TO BUY

NOTES

Date: _ _ _ _ _ / _ _

MEALS:
BREAKFAST

LUNCH

DINNER

PRIORITIES

APPOINTMENTS

WORDS TO LIVE BY

TO DO

NOTES

WATER

○ ○ ○
○ ○ ○
○ ○

CLEAN THE HOUSE

THINGS TO BUY

Date: _ _ _ _ _ / _ _

MEALS:
BREAKFAST

LUNCH

DINNER

PRIORITIES

APPOINTMENTS

WATER

◯ ◯ ◯
◯ ◯ ◯
◯ ◯

CLEAN THE HOUSE

WORDS TO LIVE BY

TO DO

THINGS TO BUY

NOTES

Date: _ _ _ _ _ / _ _

MEALS:
BREAKFAST

LUNCH

DINNER

PRIORITIES
_____
_____
_____
_____

WATER
○ ○ ○
○ ○ ○
○ ○

APPOINTMENTS
_____
_____
_____
_____

CLEAN THE HOUSE

WORDS TO LIVE BY

TO DO
_____
_____
_____
_____
_____
_____
_____

THINGS TO BUY

NOTES
_____
_____
_____
_____
_____
_____

Date: _ _ _ _ _ / _ _

MEALS:
BREAKFAST

LUNCH

DINNER

PRIORITIES

APPOINTMENTS

WATER

○ ○ ○
○ ○ ○
○ ○

CLEAN THE HOUSE

WORDS TO LIVE BY

TO DO

THINGS TO BUY

NOTES

Date: _ _ _ _ _ / _ _

MEALS:

BREAKFAST

LUNCH

DINNER

PRIORITIES

APPOINTMENTS

WATER

◯ ◯ ◯
◯ ◯ ◯
◯ ◯

CLEAN THE HOUSE

WORDS TO LIVE BY

TO DO

THINGS TO BUY

NOTES

Date: _____ / __

MEALS:
BREAKFAST

LUNCH

DINNER

PRIORITIES
_____
_____
_____
_____
_____

APPOINTMENTS
_____
_____
_____
_____

WATER
○ ○ ○
○ ○ ○
○ ○

CLEAN THE HOUSE

WORDS TO LIVE BY

TO DO
_____
_____
_____
_____
_____
_____
_____
_____
_____
_____

THINGS TO BUY

NOTES
_____
_____
_____
_____
_____
_____
_____

Date: _ _ _ _ _ / _ _

MEALS:

BREAKFAST

LUNCH

DINNER

PRIORITIES

APPOINTMENTS

WATER

○ ○ ○
○ ○ ○
○ ○

CLEAN THE HOUSE

WORDS TO LIVE BY

TO DO

THINGS TO BUY

NOTES

Date: _ _ _ _ _ / _ _

MEALS:
BREAKFAST

LUNCH

DINNER

PRIORITIES

APPOINTMENTS

WATER
◯ ◯ ◯
◯ ◯ ◯
◯ ◯

CLEAN THE HOUSE

WORDS TO LIVE BY

TO DO

THINGS TO BUY

NOTES

Date: _ _ _ _ _ / _ _

MEALS:
BREAKFAST

LUNCH

DINNER

PRIORITIES

APPOINTMENTS

WATER

○ ○ ○
○ ○ ○
○ ○

CLEAN THE HOUSE

WORDS TO LIVE BY

TO DO

THINGS TO BUY

NOTES

Date: _ _ _ _ _ / _ _

MEALS:
BREAKFAST

LUNCH

DINNER

PRIORITIES

APPOINTMENTS

TO DO

WATER

○ ○ ○
○ ○ ○
○ ○

CLEAN THE HOUSE

THINGS TO BUY

WORDS TO LIVE BY

NOTES

Date: _ _ _ _ _ / _ _

MEALS:
BREAKFAST

LUNCH

DINNER

PRIORITIES

APPOINTMENTS

WATER

○ ○ ○
○ ○ ○
○ ○

CLEAN THE HOUSE

WORDS TO LIVE BY

TO DO

THINGS TO BUY

NOTES

Date: _ _ _ _ _ / _ _

MEALS:
BREAKFAST

LUNCH

DINNER

PRIORITIES
_____
_____
_____
_____

APPOINTMENTS
_____
_____
_____
_____
_____

WATER
○ ○ ○
○ ○ ○
○ ○

CLEAN THE HOUSE

WORDS TO LIVE BY

TO DO
_____
_____
_____
_____
_____
_____
_____
_____
_____
_____
_____
_____
_____
_____

THINGS TO BUY

NOTES

Date: _ _ _ _ _ / _ _

MEALS:

BREAKFAST

LUNCH

DINNER

PRIORITIES

APPOINTMENTS

WATER

CLEAN THE HOUSE

WORDS TO LIVE BY

TO DO

THINGS TO BUY

NOTES

Date: _ _ _ _ _ / _ _

MEALS:
BREAKFAST

LUNCH

DINNER

PRIORITIES

APPOINTMENTS

WORDS TO LIVE BY

TO DO

NOTES

WATER

○ ○ ○
○ ○ ○
○ ○

CLEAN THE HOUSE

THINGS TO BUY

Date: _ _ _ _ _ / _ _

MEALS:
BREAKFAST

LUNCH

DINNER

PRIORITIES

WATER

○ ○ ○
○ ○ ○
○ ○

APPOINTMENTS

CLEAN THE HOUSE

WORDS TO LIVE BY

TO DO

THINGS TO BUY

NOTES

Date: _ _ _ _ _ / _ _

MEALS:
BREAKFAST

LUNCH

DINNER

PRIORITIES

APPOINTMENTS

WATER

○ ○ ○
○ ○ ○
○ ○

CLEAN THE HOUSE

WORDS TO LIVE BY

TO DO

THINGS TO BUY

NOTES

Date: _ _ _ _ _ / _ _

MEALS:
BREAKFAST

LUNCH

DINNER

PRIORITIES

APPOINTMENTS

WATER
◯ ◯ ◯
◯ ◯ ◯
◯ ◯

CLEAN THE HOUSE

WORDS TO LIVE BY

TO DO

THINGS TO BUY

NOTES

Date: _ _ _ _ _ / _ _

MEALS:

BREAKFAST

LUNCH

DINNER

PRIORITIES

_____
_____
_____
_____

WATER

◯ ◯ ◯
◯ ◯ ◯
◯ ◯

APPOINTMENTS

_____
_____
_____
_____

CLEAN THE HOUSE

WORDS TO LIVE BY

TO DO

_____
_____
_____
_____
_____
_____
_____
_____

THINGS TO BUY

NOTES

_____
_____
_____
_____
_____
_____

Date: _ _ _ _ _ / _ _

MEALS:

BREAKFAST

LUNCH

DINNER

PRIORITIES

APPOINTMENTS

WATER

○ ○ ○
○ ○ ○
○ ○

CLEAN THE HOUSE

WORDS TO LIVE BY

TO DO

THINGS TO BUY

NOTES

Date: _ _ _ _ _ / _ _

MEALS:
BREAKFAST

LUNCH

DINNER

PRIORITIES

APPOINTMENTS

WATER

○ ○ ○
○ ○ ○
○ ○

CLEAN
THE
HOUSE

WORDS TO
LIVE BY

TO DO

THINGS
TO BUY

NOTES

Date: _ _ _ _ _ / _ _

MEALS:
BREAKFAST

LUNCH

DINNER

PRIORITIES

APPOINTMENTS

WATER

CLEAN THE HOUSE

WORDS TO LIVE BY

TO DO

THINGS TO BUY

NOTES

Date: _ _ _ _ _ / _ _

MEALS:
BREAKFAST

LUNCH

DINNER

PRIORITIES

APPOINTMENTS

TO DO

WATER

○ ○ ○
○ ○ ○
○ ○

CLEAN THE HOUSE

THINGS TO BUY

WORDS TO LIVE BY

NOTES

Date: _ _ _ _ _ / _ _

MEALS:
BREAKFAST

LUNCH

DINNER

PRIORITIES

APPOINTMENTS

WORDS TO LIVE BY

TO DO

NOTES

WATER

○ ○ ○
○ ○ ○
○ ○

CLEAN THE HOUSE

THINGS TO BUY

Date: _____ / __

MEALS:
BREAKFAST

LUNCH

DINNER

PRIORITIES

APPOINTMENTS

WATER

◯ ◯ ◯
◯ ◯ ◯
◯ ◯

CLEAN THE HOUSE

WORDS TO LIVE BY

TO DO

THINGS TO BUY

NOTES

Date: _____ / __

MEALS:
BREAKFAST

LUNCH

DINNER

PRIORITIES

APPOINTMENTS

WORDS TO LIVE BY

TO DO

NOTES

WATER

○ ○ ○
○ ○ ○
○ ○

CLEAN THE HOUSE

THINGS TO BUY

Date: _ _ _ _ _ / _ _

MEALS:
BREAKFAST

LUNCH

DINNER

PRIORITIES

APPOINTMENTS

WATER

◯ ◯ ◯
◯ ◯ ◯
◯ ◯

CLEAN THE HOUSE

WORDS TO LIVE BY

TO DO

THINGS TO BUY

NOTES

Date: _ _ _ _ _ / _ _

MEALS:
BREAKFAST

LUNCH

DINNER

PRIORITIES
_____
_____
_____
_____

APPOINTMENTS
_____
_____
_____
_____

WATER

○ ○ ○
○ ○ ○
○ ○

CLEAN THE HOUSE

WORDS TO LIVE BY

TO DO
_____
_____
_____
_____
_____
_____
_____
_____
_____
_____
_____
_____

THINGS TO BUY

NOTES

Date: _ _ _ _ _ / _ _

MEALS:
BREAKFAST

LUNCH

DINNER

PRIORITIES

WATER

○ ○ ○
○ ○ ○
○ ○

APPOINTMENTS

CLEAN THE HOUSE

WORDS TO LIVE BY

TO DO

THINGS TO BUY

NOTES

Date: _ _ _ _ _ / _ _

MEALS:
BREAKFAST

LUNCH

DINNER

PRIORITIES

APPOINTMENTS

WORDS TO LIVE BY

TO DO

NOTES

WATER

◯ ◯ ◯
◯ ◯ ◯
◯ ◯

CLEAN THE HOUSE

THINGS TO BUY

Date: _ _ _ _ _ / _ _

MEALS:
BREAKFAST

LUNCH

DINNER

PRIORITIES

APPOINTMENTS

WORDS TO LIVE BY

TO DO

NOTES

WATER

○ ○ ○
○ ○ ○
○ ○

CLEAN THE HOUSE

THINGS TO BUY

Date: _____ / __

MEALS:

BREAKFAST

LUNCH

DINNER

PRIORITIES

APPOINTMENTS

WORDS TO LIVE BY

TO DO

NOTES

WATER

○ ○ ○
○ ○ ○
○ ○

CLEAN THE HOUSE

THINGS TO BUY

Date: _ _ _ _ _ / _ _

MEALS:
BREAKFAST

LUNCH

DINNER

PRIORITIES

APPOINTMENTS

WATER

○ ○ ○
○ ○ ○
○ ○

CLEAN THE HOUSE

WORDS TO LIVE BY

TO DO

THINGS TO BUY

NOTES

Date: _ _ _ _ _ / _ _

MEALS:
BREAKFAST

LUNCH

DINNER

PRIORITIES
_____
_____
_____
_____

APPOINTMENTS
_____
_____
_____
_____

WORDS TO LIVE BY

TO DO
_____
_____
_____
_____
_____
_____
_____

NOTES
_____
_____
_____
_____
_____
_____

WATER
○ ○ ○
○ ○ ○
○ ○

CLEAN THE HOUSE

THINGS TO BUY

Date: _ _ _ _ _ / _ _

PRIORITIES

MEALS:

BREAKFAST

LUNCH

DINNER

WATER

○ ○ ○
○ ○ ○
○ ○

APPOINTMENTS

CLEAN
THE
HOUSE

WORDS TO
LIVE BY

TO DO

THINGS
TO BUY

NOTES

Date: _ _ _ _ _ / _ _

MEALS:

BREAKFAST

LUNCH

DINNER

PRIORITIES

_____
_____
_____
_____

APPOINTMENTS

_____
_____
_____
_____

WATER

○ ○ ○
○ ○ ○
○ ○

CLEAN THE HOUSE

WORDS TO LIVE BY

TO DO

_____
_____
_____
_____
_____
_____
_____
_____
_____
_____
_____
_____
_____
_____
_____

THINGS TO BUY

NOTES

Date: _____ / __

MEALS:
BREAKFAST

LUNCH

DINNER

WORDS TO LIVE BY

NOTES

PRIORITIES

APPOINTMENTS

TO DO

WATER

○ ○ ○
○ ○ ○
○ ○

CLEAN THE HOUSE

THINGS TO BUY

Date: _ _ _ _ _ / _ _

MEALS:
BREAKFAST

LUNCH

DINNER

PRIORITIES

APPOINTMENTS

WATER

○ ○ ○
○ ○ ○
○ ○

CLEAN THE HOUSE

WORDS TO LIVE BY

TO DO

THINGS TO BUY

NOTES

Date: _ _ _ _ _ / _ _

PRIORITIES

MEALS:

BREAKFAST

_____

_____

LUNCH

_____

DINNER

APPOINTMENTS

_____

_____

_____

WATER

○ ○ ○
○ ○ ○
○ ○

CLEAN THE HOUSE

WORDS TO LIVE BY

TO DO

_____

_____

_____

_____

_____

_____

_____

NOTES

_____

_____

_____

_____

_____

_____

THINGS TO BUY

Date: _____ / __

MEALS:

BREAKFAST

LUNCH

DINNER

PRIORITIES

_____
_____
_____
_____

APPOINTMENTS

_____
_____
_____
_____

WATER

○ ○ ○
○ ○ ○
○ ○

**CLEAN
THE
HOUSE**

**WORDS TO
LIVE BY**

TO DO

_____
_____
_____
_____
_____
_____
_____
_____

**THINGS
TO BUY**

NOTES

_____
_____
_____
_____
_____
_____
_____

Date: _ _ _ _ _ / _ _

MEALS:
BREAKFAST

LUNCH

DINNER

PRIORITIES
_____
_____
_____
_____

APPOINTMENTS
_____
_____
_____
_____

WATER
○ ○ ○
○ ○ ○
○ ○

CLEAN THE HOUSE

WORDS TO LIVE BY

TO DO
_____
_____
_____
_____
_____
_____
_____
_____

THINGS TO BUY

NOTES
_____
_____
_____
_____
_____

Date: _ _ _ _ _ / _ _

MEALS:

BREAKFAST

LUNCH

DINNER

PRIORITIES

WATER

○ ○ ○
○ ○ ○
○ ○

APPOINTMENTS

CLEAN THE HOUSE

WORDS TO LIVE BY

TO DO

THINGS TO BUY

NOTES

Date: _ _ _ _ _ / _ _

MEALS:
BREAKFAST

LUNCH

DINNER

PRIORITIES

APPOINTMENTS

WATER

○ ○ ○
○ ○ ○
○ ○

CLEAN THE HOUSE

WORDS TO LIVE BY

TO DO

THINGS TO BUY

NOTES

Date: _____ / __

MEALS:
BREAKFAST

LUNCH

DINNER

PRIORITIES

WATER
○ ○ ○
○ ○ ○
○ ○

APPOINTMENTS

CLEAN THE HOUSE

WORDS TO LIVE BY

TO DO

THINGS TO BUY

NOTES

Date: _____ / __

MEALS:
BREAKFAST

LUNCH

DINNER

PRIORITIES

APPOINTMENTS

WORDS TO LIVE BY

TO DO

NOTES

WATER

○ ○ ○
○ ○ ○
○ ○

CLEAN THE HOUSE

THINGS TO BUY

Date: _____ / __

MEALS:
BREAKFAST

LUNCH

DINNER

PRIORITIES
_____
_____
_____
_____
_____

APPOINTMENTS
_____
_____
_____

WATER
○ ○ ○
○ ○ ○
○ ○

CLEAN THE HOUSE

WORDS TO LIVE BY

TO DO
_____
_____
_____
_____
_____
_____
_____
_____

THINGS TO BUY

NOTES
_____
_____
_____
_____
_____
_____

Date: _ _ _ _ _ / _ _

MEALS:
BREAKFAST

LUNCH

DINNER

PRIORITIES

APPOINTMENTS

TO DO

WORDS TO LIVE BY

NOTES

WATER

○ ○ ○
○ ○ ○
○ ○

CLEAN THE HOUSE

THINGS TO BUY

Date: _ _ _ _ _ / _ _

MEALS:
BREAKFAST

LUNCH

DINNER

PRIORITIES

APPOINTMENTS

WATER

○ ○ ○
○ ○ ○
○ ○

CLEAN THE HOUSE

WORDS TO LIVE BY

TO DO

THINGS TO BUY

NOTES

Date: _ _ _ _ _ / _ _

MEALS:
BREAKFAST

LUNCH

DINNER

PRIORITIES

APPOINTMENTS

WORDS TO LIVE BY

TO DO

NOTES

WATER

◯ ◯ ◯
◯ ◯ ◯
◯ ◯

CLEAN THE HOUSE

THINGS TO BUY

Date: _ _ _ _ _ / _ _

PRIORITIES

MEALS:

BREAKFAST

LUNCH

DINNER

APPOINTMENTS

WATER

○ ○ ○
○ ○ ○
○ ○

CLEAN THE HOUSE

WORDS TO LIVE BY

TO DO

THINGS TO BUY

NOTES

Date: _ _ _ _ _ / _ _

MEALS:
BREAKFAST

LUNCH

DINNER

PRIORITIES

APPOINTMENTS

WORDS TO LIVE BY

TO DO

NOTES

WATER
○ ○ ○
○ ○ ○
○ ○

CLEAN THE HOUSE

THINGS TO BUY

Date: _ _ _ _ _ / _ _

MEALS:
BREAKFAST

LUNCH

DINNER

PRIORITIES

APPOINTMENTS

WATER

◯ ◯ ◯
◯ ◯ ◯
◯ ◯

CLEAN THE HOUSE

WORDS TO LIVE BY

TO DO

THINGS TO BUY

NOTES

Date: _ _ _ _ _ / _ _

MEALS:
BREAKFAST

LUNCH

DINNER

PRIORITIES

APPOINTMENTS

WATER

○ ○ ○
○ ○ ○
○ ○

CLEAN
THE
HOUSE

WORDS TO
LIVE BY

TO DO

THINGS
TO BUY

NOTES

Made in the USA
Middletown, DE
09 December 2021